THE MAGNA CARTA CHRO

1215 to 2015: a special report on 800 years in the fight for freedom

By our political staff Christopher Lloyd and Patrick Skipworth

King's fate sealed at Runnymede

From our royal correspondent,
Runnymede, June 16, 1215

Challenge to absolute power of the King to raise taxes is issued by barons fed up with financing royal wars

A RADICAL NEW set of laws forbidding the King from exercising divine right over his subjects was sealed yesterday on the banks of the River Thames.

Armour-clad barons, fed up with the King's repeated demands for more money and soldiers, were waiting for King John as he returned from a series of disastrous wars in France. Yesterday's confrontation follows a dispute in May this year when the Mayor of the City of London ordered that

the City gates be opened to rebels who subsequently took control of key royal assets such as the Treasury.

King John met rebel barons yesterday at Runnymede, neutral ground between Windsor and London, to negotiate a settlement. It is not clear exactly who drew up the new charter although inside sources suggest that Archbishop Stephen Langton, who has studied similar manuscripts, played a part in the drafting.

While every King of England since William the Conqueror's Norman invasion of 1066 has faced rebellions, the barons' recent demands include a call for new laws and freedoms for England, although they do not propose any replacement for royal authority.

King John was excommunicated from the Catholic Church only six years ago, following arguments with Pope Innocent III. A major fire which broke out in London in

1212 has been called a bad omen of the King's unholy rule. Although readmitted into the Church in 1213, many say that King John's reputation has never recovered in the eyes of his people.

Several copies of the new charter have been made. Messengers are presently dispatching them across the country so that the charter will remain a symbol for posterity, showing that the King's powers are not absolute. However, it remains to be seen whether the King will honour the new rules or if England will see fresh friction break out between the King and his barons.

What's special about this new charter?

THE BARONS' CHARTER is the first document to stipulate some limitations on the power and prerogative of the King.

One clause states that the King cannot raise taxes without the consent of earls, barons and bishops at a formal meeting. The charter also states that freedoms must be granted by the barons to England's lower classes.

Perhaps most importantly, in an effort to protect further against John's poor rule, the charter establishes a council of 25 barons who can overrule

the will of the King if he breaks the new charter.

Some commentators say it marks the beginning of a new era in which rulers are ultimately subject to the laws of the realm.

It is also significant that so many copies of the new charter have been made by scribes. Messengers have been dispatched far and wide to display the new charter in cities as far flung as Salisbury, Hereford, Durham and Worcester so ordinary people can see its provisions for themselves.

De Montfort's parliament reaffirms sanctity of Magna Carta

By our Westminster staff,
January 21, 1265

A GROUND-BREAKING meeting was held yesterday by Simon de Montfort and his band of barons.

Having captured the King at the Battle of Lewes last year, the revolutionary baron, de Montfort, yesterday called an emergency gathering which is being hailed as England's first-ever 'representative parliament'.

For the first time in such a meeting elected representatives from England's major towns were invited to participate. Critics are divided on whether this representative system, which may see more power devolved into the hands of ordinary English people, will catch on.

The special meeting follows an earlier attempt in Oxford by de Montfort to reinstate some of the changes brought about by

The Barons' Charter of 1215, now known simply as Magna Carta, which King Henry III has repeatedly ignored, leading to the current crisis.

Yesterday's meeting enforced a legal obligation on the King to respect his subjects' rights and to involve his people in political decisions. The charters drawn up in these meetings have been published in English, leaving behind the little-spoken languages of Latin and French.

Black Death gives peasants power to demand more pay

By our medical correspondent, London, July 3, 1349

IN AN EXTRAORDINARY twist of fate, many survivors of the dreadful plague known as the 'Black Death' are finding that their situations have actually improved since the disease took hold.

The plague, which arrived in England last year, has caused the gruesome deaths of millions. London has lost up to two-thirds of its inhabitants. Victims are being buried on top of each other because graveyards can no longer cope. The terrifying disease, which manifests as foul lumps in the groin and armpits, finally causes the death of more than half of those infected within three days.

However, for those unharmed by the plague things are looking up. The widespread loss of life has turned aristocrats' estates into ghost towns and villages. With no one to bring in the harvests, estate owners are offering peasants across the country higher wages to move to their farms and work for them. Land has become plentiful, making it cheaper than ever for peasants to purchase a place of their own.

Such changes are leading to a shift in the social make-up with more peasants throwing off their feudal ties, owning their own properties and earning good wages. The vanishing towns and villages are also causing peasants to flock to the cities despite the increased danger of plague. Abandoned farms are turning back into forests and wildernesses. Some are calling this the end of England's feudal system now that peasants and their descendants are having the opportunity to decide the directions of their own lives.

Caxton's press ushers in new information age

By our industrial correspondent, London, January 5, 1480

A BRILLIANT INVENTION from Europe has been brought to England by renowned merchant and writer William Caxton.

The printing press is a mechanical machine which uses small metal letters arranged into words to print pages at a rapid speed. Caxton claims his press can print thousands of pages every day transforming the labours of traditional hand-copyists who struggle to produce only a few. Caxton is predicting that the invention will bring about a revolution in reading across Europe and the world.

Invention of the new moveable-type printing press is claimed by German goldsmith Johannes Gutenberg. He got the idea for the screw press from similar presses used to crush grapes for wine.

Caxton first came across Gutenberg's press on a trip to the German city of Cologne. Whilst living in Belgium and following the growing popularity of the French novel, *The Recuyell of the Historyes of Troye*, Caxton decided to get a press of his own. This romance, printed by Caxton using his new press, is the first book ever printed in English.

Caxton is now making plans for his next book. His press has already produced Chaucer's famous *Canterbury Tales*. Sources close to Caxton suggest he is working on a new version of the legendary story of King Arthur's life and death.

Besides legends and stories, many scientists and philosophers are also excited about the changes the new press will bring. With the ability to print their works quickly and cheaply, they will be able to compare notes and share ideas across the world more easily.

Hopes are high that the availability of mass-produced books will open the floodgates to a new world of learning and education for all people.

OK! WORSHIP WHAT YOU LIKE SAYS HENRY IV

By our religious affairs editor, Nantes, May 1, 1598

THE FRENCH KING last night issued a royal decree promising his people the freedom to follow whatever religion they want without fear of persecution and violence. King Henry hopes his dramatic intervention will bring an end to violent religious wars that have plagued France for more than a generation.

For over thirty years France has been gripped by vicious religious warfare between Catholics and Huguenot Protestants, members of a new Christian movement based on the radical ideas of the late French reformer, John Calvin.

But yesterday, in a dramatic volte-face, Henry IV, King of France, issued an edict from the French city of Nantes, promising the Huguenots religious freedom and protection from persecution.

Observers say the spirit of religious toleration in France could be the start of a new era of religious freedoms throughout the whole of Europe.

American colonies given 'Magna Carta' liberties

By our colonies correspondent,
Jamestown, November 19, 1618

SETTLERS in Jamestown, Virginia, the first permanent English-speaking colony in the New World, were yesterday granted land ownership rights and their own democratic assembly. All free men living on the frontier will also have the right to vote for their own political leaders.

The colony, which lies on the east coast of America, was founded at Jamestown in 1607. English settlers were sent by the Virginia Company after it received a royal charter to colonise parts of the New World in 1606. The original charter granted those living and born in the colony the 'same rights as English citizens elsewhere'. Hopes were high that bringing such liberties, which have their origins in Magna Carta, to the New World may help stimulate a flourishing new settlement.

However, the colony has been beset by disputes amongst leaders, disease and a lack of supplies, causing it rapidly to shrink in population. In desperation, the Virginia Company turned to leading English lawyer Sir Edwin Sandys to draft the recent charter.

Sandys hopes that additional freedoms for the settlers may help new settlements in the New World to flourish. Greater autonomy will give colonists responsibility for making their own decisions, especially when it comes to choosing which crops to grow and trade.

The strategy is aimed at encouraging more people to settle in the New World colonies.

Habeas Corpus Bill numbers almost too close to call

May 28, 1679, Westminster, London

AFTER A NAIL-BITING session in the House of Lords last night, King Charles II has given his royal assent to a new Act of Parliament which will ensure nobody is ever detained unlawfully and without proper trial.

The Habeas Corpus Act entitles any prisoner to make a demand on their own or someone else's behalf to have the legality of their imprisonment examined by a judge. If their imprisonment is legal then they have the right to a trial, if not they are to be set free.

The new law is designed to prevent cruel jailers, sheriffs or even private citizens simply imprisoning people they don't like, since it allows them to request a fair trial.

Rumours are circulating that one Lord 'cheated' the counting system to get the Act passed. Lord Grey, who was counting those in favour of the Act, apparently counted an especially overweight Lord as ten Lords and Lord Norris, who was supposed to be watching him, then failed to notice. True or false, the Act is now enshrined into English law.

The Earl of Shaftesbury, who first put forward the Act, is known for his opposition to the Catholic James becoming the next King of England and some believe this Act is intended to prevent the future King James ruling arbitrarily.

Europe agrees on principles of national self-determination

By our diplomatic editor, Münster, Holy Roman Empire, October 25, 1648

A NEW TREATY signed by Europe's major powers is destined to bring to an end thirty years of bitter European war as well as reshuffle the balance of power between countries across the continent. The Treaty of Westphalia forces all German princes to respect one another's religious beliefs and those of their subjects.

Germany has long been a battleground for the Catholics, Lutherans and Calvinists of Europe to fight religious wars. Commentators say the new treaty should help end these lengthy conflicts.

The rights given to Lutheran and Calvinist Protestants, both viewed as heretics by the Catholic Church, will greatly dilute the power of Catholicism in Europe.

Pope Innocent X is understood to have serious misgivings about the treaty, which, according to insiders, he says is "null, void, invalid, iniquitous, unjust, damnable, reprobate, inane, empty of meaning and effect for all time".

It is thought that formal recognition of the more religiously tolerant Dutch Republic should also make Europe a safer place for Jews to live in.

The treaty also encourages European states to avoid meddling in one another's affairs, and requires mutual respect for 'territorial integrity'.

It is hoped that these measures will prevent power-hungry kings and princes from setting their eyes upon one another's lands. They are also designed to encourage people to choose their nations' leaders for themselves.

Up to a third of Germany's population has been decimated by the wars which began in 1618 after two Catholic diplomats were thrown out of a window by Protestants at a council meeting in Prague.

English Bill of Rights guarantees petitions, free speech and elections

By our Westminster editor, London, December 17, 1689

MAJOR NEW LAWS granting important freedoms to Parliament and the people of England were passed yesterday in Westminster.

England's new 'Bill of Rights' will allow MPs to speak freely in Parliament without fear of punishment.

It will also prevent King William and Queen Mary from meddling in elections so that their favourites get in, making Parliament a safe haven for England's citizens and their representatives to discuss issues freely and without fear of reprisal.

Political commentators say the Act has been inspired by the ideas of the English philosopher John Locke, who places individual freedom at the centre of society's purpose.

The Act should also protect against autocratic royal antics, as practised by the previous king, James II, who was well known for imprisoning people who spoke out against him.

Additionally, the Act restates that laws and taxes require the consent of the English people through their representatives in Parliament. It also opens up a closer line of communication between monarchs and their people – allowing anyone to petition the King and Queen on important issues without fear of punishment or reprisal.

Bassi made first woman professor

BRILLIANT ITALIAN SCIENTIST Laura Bassi has become Europe's first female professor. Dr Bassi has taken up her post as Professor of Anatomy at the University of Bologna, Europe's oldest university. Dr Bassi's appointment represents both a major success for women's rights and for scientific research on the continent. Dr Bassi is also an expert in the ideas of the late Sir Isaac Newton, the talented English physicist well known for his theory of gravity.

US Declaration grants unalienable rights to 'all men'

Founding Fathers agree on universal principles meant to bind all humanity

By our US bureau, July 5, 1776

THE THIRTEEN AMERICAN colonies yesterday marked their independence from Britain with a Declaration outlining the right of all men to "life, liberty and the pursuit of happiness" as the cornerstone of their proposed new nation. The colonies officially declared independence three days ago.

The Declaration has been drafted by Thomas Jefferson, an outspoken proponent of democracy and individual liberty. The document contains many powerful statements regarding the natural rights owed to all of mankind which, claims Mr Jefferson, governments are duty-bound to protect and uphold.

The Declaration also states that it is the duty of a people "to alter or to abolish" a despotic government. This duty, according to Mr Jefferson, legitimises the current ongoing war of independence between Britain and the American colonies.

Some are calling this new charter a 'right to revolution' which may be traced back to Magna Carta which attempted to establish supervisory powers over any monarch to ensure they rule with an appropriate level of consultation with their people.

Revolutionary ideas such as these have been reinforced in recent times with the works of

philosophers such as Englishman John Locke who argued for the "natural liberty of man". Perhaps the most revolutionary aspect of the new Declaration is the notion that "all men are created equal". It is not yet clear as to what extent the new nation will embrace this idea, given its large slave population.

Mr Jefferson has already expressed his anger that a passage opposing the slave trade has been removed by others involved in the drafting process. Some have also noted the decidedly male focus of the document – perhaps "all men and all women are created equal" would have been more egalitarian.

The majority of the text is devoted to outlining the American colonies' reasons for independence, specifically the "repeated injuries and usurpations" suffered under the "absolute tyranny" of King George III.

One of the biggest complaints of the American people has been regarding their lack of representation within the British Parliament, despite being taxpayers with the same obligations as any other Englishman. The current war was triggered by a group protesting about taxes paid on the import of tea. Other grievances, such as depriving Americans of the right to trial by jury, are also mentioned in the new Declaration.

Liberté, Égalité, Fraternité!

By our Paris correspondent, June 26, 1793

A HISTORIC DAY was marked across France yesterday as nearly two million French citizens turned out to vote on a new constitution proclaiming the right of each individual to equality and freedom.

The vote follows years of bloody revolution against the excessive power of the French King and aristocracy.

Political upheavals began four years ago when members of the Third Estate (the common people) were barred from an official meeting with the King. Instead, they gathered in a nearby tennis court and swore not to rest until the people had taken back power for themselves.

Although hopes are high this new egalitarian government will help solve France's problems of debt, poverty and famine, the Revolution has already been long, violent and chaotic. Many French aristocrats and citizens, including the King, have lost their lives to the revolutionaries' weapon of choice: the gruesome guillotine – a long, falling blade which delivers a quick, clean chop to the neck.

Great Reform Bill is a nail in the coffin for rotten boroughs

By our politics editor, June 8, 1832

HUNDREDS OF THOUSANDS of previously disenfranchised British citizens will now have the right to vote.

Parliament yesterday passed the Representation of the People Act which will extend the right to have a say in government to roughly one in five of all adult males.

The Act also provides representation for many people living in new towns that have sprung up as a result of the Industrial Revolution.

Until now some MPs have represented thousands of voters, while other constituencies, known as 'rotten boroughs', have MPs elected by less than ten!

Old Sarum in Wiltshire has two MPs but only seven voters and three houses in the constituency. Meanwhile, Liverpool has one MP, but has an electorate of more than 11,000.

Other constituencies can be controlled by one wealthy patron who may also own the houses of a small group of voters, dominating them as a strict landlord.

The Duke of Newcastle has been said to have seven of these 'pocket boroughs', so called because he has them 'in his pocket', ready to do his bidding.

By making laws granting people the right to vote the same across the country, a much larger portion of the UK's population will now be represented in elections.

But some are clamouring for all men over the age of 21, regardless of status or wealth, to be allowed to vote. They are set to carry on petitioning the King and his government until their demands are met.

Bolívar's freedom crusade sweeps through South American colonies

By our South America correspondent, Bogotá, Colombia, June 24, 1821

CELEBRATIONS are reverberating across South America following Simón Bolívar's heroic campaigns to deliver independence for the continent from the Kingdom of Spain.

'El Libertador', as he is now being called, has fought against Spanish rule for over a decade, leading armies in Venezuela, Colombia and Ecuador and helping to establish the new Republic of Gran Colombia.

The independence movement has developed as South Americans have watched the birth of new republics in France and the USA, demanding similar liberties in a bid to throw out their European overlords.

Simultaneously, Spanish power has been weakening following disastrous wars against Napoleon in Europe and declining wealth from New World silver and gold mines.

Anger is still simmering after the King of Spain, Fernando VII, rejected proposals for a revised Spanish constitution in 1812 which would have given new rights and opportunities for Spanish and South American citizens.

The independence movement also marks the start of a campaign for the liberation of slaves in South America. Bolívar is well known as a strict opponent of and campaigner against slavery. Measures are now under way to ban slavery in these new South American states.

At last! Slavery banned across the Empire

Dream comes true for recently deceased MP William Wilberforce

By our political editor, Westminster, August 29, 1833

SUPPORTERS of the abolitionist cause were cock-a-hoop last night as Britain finally declared slavery illegal throughout the Empire. The success follows nearly fifty long years of campaigning and builds upon an earlier law from 1807 which banned the trade and transport of slaves. Yesterday's law will turn hundreds of thousands of slaves across the Empire into free men and women.

Although people of all different backgrounds and political parties have rallied around the issue, the most notable campaigner of all was the late Mr William Wilberforce, formerly Member of Parliament for Yorkshire. A highly religious man driven by a strong sense of

morals, Mr Wilberforce provided a constant and powerful voice within Parliament in support of the abolitionist movement. Despite numerous bouts of debilitating illness which, tragically, claimed his life only last month, Mr

Wilberforce was a vociferous supporter of abolition for the forty years up to his death. He once famously described slavery as a "bloody traffic" which future generations will see as "a disgrace and dishonour to this country".

The British government intends to pay £20 million in compensation to slave owners across Britain and the Empire.

The Bishop of Exeter, Henry Phillpotts, has been promised the massive sum of £12,700 as compensation for freeing 665 slaves who worked on his plantation in Barbados. The bishop is apparently already making plans to use the money to refurbish his mansion in Torquay.

Despite the banning of slave trading across the British Empire in 1807, slavery still exists on a large scale in the USA. A deep divide is developing between US states which allow and those which forbid slavery. A substantial number of people in the southern US work as slaves on cotton plantations, often in appalling conditions.

MILL'S BOOK IS A BOON FOR LIBERTY

By our literary editor, Avignon, 1859

NOTHING LESS than total gender equality will do, according to philosopher John Stuart Mill in his latest book, On Liberty.

Mill also says that to protect individual freedom, limits must be set on the power of the state. His book discusses what these limits should be.

Commentators claim that Mill's new book raises important issues for citizens everywhere since in today's democratic countries, even without the absolute power of monarchs and aristocrats, the threat of tyrannical government still remains.

Mill cites his late wife, Harriet Taylor Mill, as a co-author of On Liberty, *saying that she helped him develop many of his ground-breaking opinions. He has published it to "consecrate it to her memory".*

Mill currently lives in Avignon, France, but many are wondering whether it is time for this stalwart proponent of liberty to set his sights on Parliament and begin campaigning to turn his ideas into reality.

US Civil War finally ends as Good ol' South submits to a ban on slaves

By our US editor, April 10, 1865

THE MONUMENTAL WAR which has engulfed the United States for nearly four years has at last come to an end following victory for the Union.

Confederate States of America general Robert E. Lee yesterday surrendered to Union general Ulysses S. Grant effectively bringing the bloody conflict to a close. As a result, the United States will endure and slavery will end for good in the South.

Despite the United States Constitution placing the protection of individual liberty as a chief concern of the government and a right of all people, the country has the largest population of slaves of any nation. The 1860 census recorded 4 million slaves.

The Civil War's origins largely stem from this contradiction. Following the election of pro-abolitionist Abraham Lincoln as President, 11 states seceded from the Union and formed the Confederate States of America. Southern states feared abolition would

destroy their cotton-based economies that traditionally depend on slave labour for commercial success.

While Lincoln's original purpose for the war was restoring the Union, the focus shifted to ending slavery following his 'Emancipation Proclamation' on January 1, 1863, which proclaimed the freedom of all slaves in the rebellious states.

Historians are already calling the conflict the first-ever 'industrial war' since modern technology such as railroads, mass production and the telegraph machine has been used

throughout. This new technology has led to more destruction, making this the bloodiest war in America's history with more than 600,000 lives lost.

A motion to make slavery a criminal act is now making its way through Congress.

Observers say that the mindset of the American people has been changed permanently by the traumatic events of the Civil War, although some fear that political uncertainty could still last well into the future.

Children to be educated at school 'or otherwise'

Reading, writing and maths available for all

By our education correspondent, February 18, 1870

THOUSANDS of new schools are to be opened across the country after Parliament yesterday voted to take children out of the fields and factories and put them into compulsory education.

Whilst employers are worried about losing an important element of the workforce to the schools, supporters of the new Education Act say it will make British workers the most skilled in the world, unlocking countless opportunities for future generations.

Yesterday's vote means all children between the ages of five and 13 will be required to be in education. It is hoped that the measure will enable Britain to be at the forefront of global intellectual and artistic development by virtue of having a younger generation that will be largely literate.

The Act, however, does not specify how or where children must be educated. It merely sets out a series of standards. A House of Lords amendment allows a child's education to take place at school 'or otherwise'. The provision means that parents who do not wish their children to mix with others of a different social status at a Church or private school may educate them at home instead.

Some worry that the system may lead to vastly different standards of education, with some people receiving far better or worse teaching than others, while the upper classes may choose to segregate their children from the rest. Additionally, the Act does not provide free education, although help will be given to particularly poor families.

However, the loss of child labour, which often provides a significant portion of a poor household's income, may make it increasingly hard for many hard-working families to make ends meet.

The new law has been championed mainly by members of the Liberal Party who hope to promote further freedom of choice, social mobility and opportunity for individuals, regardless of class or status, through social reforms.

As a result of the Reform Act, which gave the vote to a vast number of largely illiterate citizens three years ago, government insiders believe that education will be essential for ensuring people can cast their votes intelligently.

Robert Lowe, Chancellor of the Exchequer, said that it was the duty of Parliament "to compel our future masters to learn their letters".

Mr William Gladstone, current Liberal Prime Minister of the UK, is well known for his support for social mobility, something he strongly believes can be achieved through universal education. He claims the new Act will help throw off constraints on poor people – fixing an injustice originating from Britain's aristocratic past.

House of Commons makes itself supreme

By our politics editor, Westminster, August 19, 1911

AFTER MANY failed attempts and following years of debate, Britain's Liberal MPs have finally managed to pass their Parliament Act into law. The new Act severely limits the ability of the House of Lords to make or break a new law in Britain, giving the elected House of Commons the power to govern largely unopposed.

Whilst the House of Lords cannot create new laws, traditionally it must give its assent to pass those created in the Commons. This has made the passing of the Parliament Act especially difficult, since it means the House of Lords having to grant its assent to a new law which restricts its own power.

It took the King threatening to create numerous new Liberal Lords just to get the Act through, causing the Opposition to back down. The Act will allow the current Liberal government to make a series of important social welfare reforms which, now the Lords are not able to block them, should dramatically improve ordinary people's lives.

The driving force behind the current initiative is the Chancellor of the Exchequer David Lloyd George, who, in a bid to reduce inequality, has been campaigning hard to introduce a new tax on wealthy landowners. However, he has found himself repeatedly blocked from passing the bill by Conservatives in the House of Lords, many of whom would be victims of the new tax.

Breaking the grip of the House of Lords, whose members are not elected but are appointed by Ministers, represents more than just a victory for Mr Lloyd George and the Liberals. It extends a fundamental element underpinning Britain's claim to be a free and democratic country.

Statue of Liberty welcomes all

HUNDREDS OF THOUSANDS of New Yorkers took to the streets yesterday to celebrate the unveiling of a spectacular new statue representing American freedom and values. The new monument is a joint project between France and the USA, acknowledging a shared belief in equal rights and opportunities.

Sculptor Frédéric-Auguste Bartholdi and engineer Gustave Eiffel have spent more than a decade building the statue which depicts Libertas, the Roman goddess of freedom. It has been erected on Bedloe Island in the city's harbour in the hope that arriving immigrants will be inspired by its powerful message.

Suffragette is killed by King's horse at Epsom races

By our racing reporter, June 9, 1913

EMILY DAVISON, described as a militant suffragette, died in hospital yesterday following injuries sustained after colliding with the King's horse, Anmer, at the Epsom Derby last week.

Miss Davison was knocked unconscious by the horse after she stepped out in front of it during the race. A doctor, who hurried to the scene, restored her pulse on the racetrack by applying a hot-tea-soaked handkerchief to her wrist. But, yesterday, the suffragette died after failing to recover from a major skull fracture and numerous internal injuries.

Miss Davison, who was a member of the controversial Women's Social and Political Union, was well known for using aggressive tactics to raise awareness for women's suffering and devoted much of her life to the 'Votes for

Women' movement. Although her actions put her in trouble with the law, resulting in nine prison sentences, her passion for the movement was never broken.

Witness reports of the incident provide little insight as to what were Miss Davison's real intentions.

John Ervine, who witnessed the incident, is adamant that her actions were deliberate. "I feel sure that Miss Davison meant to stop the horse," he said. Others said she merely intended to hold up the race. Yet more have suggested that she tried to attach the purple, white and green suffragette flags she was carrying to the King's horse,

Anmer. The horse would then have crossed the finishing line wearing the three colours of the suffragette movement, which represent dignity, purity and hope.

The King immediately enquired about the condition of his jockey, Mr Jones, following the incident, but has given little other response. The Queen Mother, however, is known to have sent a messenger to the hospital to enquire as to Miss Davison's condition, although, in a telegram to Mr Jones, she lamented the "sad accident caused through the abominable conduct of a brutal lunatic woman".

Many are calling Miss Davison more of a madwoman than a martyr and see her actions as a direct insult to the Royal Family. Regardless, the incident has raised significant awareness of the suffragette movement across the country, a legacy of which Miss Davison would surely approve.

POPE INSPIRES WORKERS TO DEMAND MORE RIGHTS

By our religious affairs editor, Vatican City, May 16, 1891

THE POPE has thrown down the gauntlet to employers, demanding they must improve the livelihood of badly treated workers across the Catholic world and beyond.

In a letter issued to his bishops yesterday, Pope Leo XIII encourages growing trade union movements that are fighting for the right of workers to organise themselves into 'unions' to achieve better working conditions.

Unions are becoming increasingly political and, here in the UK, the Pope's message will lend support to the creation of a political labour party dedicated to the workers' cause.

The Pope said there was a "misery and wretchedness pressing so unjustly on the majority of the working class" due to the awful conditions many poor people are now working under.

Lawrence's plan for Islamic freedom is spiked

By our Middle East editor, November 27, 1917

A SECRET DOCUMENT leaked by the new Russian Socialist state has revealed the uncomfortable truth behind Britain and France's plans for the Middle East.

The Sykes–Picot treaty, which was intended to be kept hidden away from prying eyes until the end of the war, outlines Britain and France's intention to carve up the area of the Middle East known as 'Greater Syria'. The treaty apparently scuttles hopes for a unified Arabic state.

According to the document, Syria, Lebanon and parts of Iraq will be managed by France, while Britain will control Jordan and southern Iraq.

Russia had originally been included in the treaty, but the other two powers have refused to accept the legitimacy of the new Communist government. This disagreement is what may have led to the surprise release of the secret document by the Russians yesterday.

The announcement is awkward for the British who have depended on the military support of the Arab people in the war. In return, it was

widely assumed that after the war is over the Arab people would be granted sovereign independence. Officials are concerned that after yesterday's disclosure the Arabs will now refuse to support Britian's bid to defeat the vast Ottoman Empire.

Until now trust between the British and the Arabs has been gradually established thanks to the extraordinary efforts of British

Colonel T.E. Lawrence, a former archaeologist who became a close friend and military adviser to Arab leaders fighting against the oppressive Ottoman Empire.

The Sharif of Mecca has even given Lawrence the status of one of his own sons.

Despite news of the secret agreement, Lawrence is thought to be organising a new offensive into the Ottoman province of Syria.

Women get same voting rights as men at last!

By our parliamentary correspondent, Westminster, July 3, 1928

THE LONG STRUGGLE for women's suffrage has finally come to an end as yesterday a parliamentary bill became law giving equal voting rights to both men and women aged 21 and over.

Supporters of women's suffrage were celebrating last night, ten years after a law was passed which granted the vote to all women over 30, who met certain requirements, while the male vote was extended to all men over 21.

Commentators believe the historic discrepancy between ages for male and female voters may have been intended to prevent women having a huge majority amongst British voters, following the many male casualties in the First World War.

Almost two years after this law was passed Nancy Astor, elected Tory MP for Plymouth Sutton in 1919, became the first woman ever to take a seat in Parliament.

Yesterday's announcement of the new equal votes law comes only weeks after the death of Mrs Emmeline Pankhurst, a passionate member and central figure of the women's suffrage movement which has existed for over half a century.

Mrs Pankhurst's contribution to the suffragettes lives on in her daughters, Christabel and Sylvia, who are both involved with the campaign for equal votes.

The movement has been well known for its up-front and confrontational methods, including vandalising property and undergoing hunger strikes in protest against imprisonment.

Following the new law, it is expected that woman will make up 52.7 per cent of the electorate, representing a major shift in the balance of power in politics.

Supporters of universal suffrage believe the new rules will make governments more representative of the wishes of the population.

President lays down four freedoms: Speech, Religion, Want and Fear

By our US editor, Washington, January 7, 1941

PRESIDENT ROOSEVELT last night made clear his own personal allegiance to the Allied cause by championing democracy across the world in the face of global fascism. His words come despite his country's official neutrality in the Second World War.

In this year's 'State of the Union' address, the President proposed four freedoms to which people "everywhere in the world" have rights. Nations which enjoy liberty had a duty to protect them, he added.

Roosevelt referred to the significant threat posed by fascist powers to all democratic nations, including the USA. His speech indicated that America might aid the Allies in the fight against fascism, perhaps signalling an end to the USA's isolationist policy.

In his landmark address, Roosevelt described the freedom of speech, freedom of religion, freedom from want and freedom from fear as human liberties which all people should be able to enjoy. He said these liberties were "no vision of a distant millennium", but "attainable in our own time and generation".

The President went on to describe these four freedoms as the "antithesis" of the so-called new order of tyranny which dictators such as Adolf Hitler are in the process of trying to create. His words clearly outline his wish for a democratic victory in the war.

Yesterday's presidential address was not without its critics, however. Isolationists, worried by Roosevelt's increasingly bellicose rhetoric, were quick to find fault with it, as were conservatives who viewed the speech simply as another part of Roosevelt's push for social reforms and greater government control.

BRETTON BANKERS AGREE DEAL

DELEGATES from 44 different Allied nations have come to an agreement regarding the future of the world's economies, writes our US correspondent, July 23, 1944.

As the Second World War continues, many of the Allied nations believe that the economic hardship suffered across the globe following the First World War played a major role in the rise of fascism and the Axis powers they are currently fighting.

The agreement sets out ways a similar economic downturn can be avoided by supporting free trade and ensuring poverty is alleviated through international aid arrangements for poorer states.

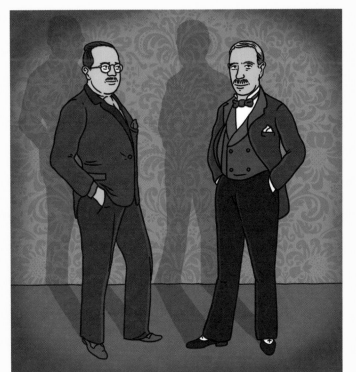

UN agrees Human Rights charter, a 'Magna Carta' for the modern age

Vote passes with 48 nations in favour and 8 abstensions

By our United Nations correspondent, December 11, 1948

A NEW 'MAGNA CARTA for all humanity' was signed into international law yesterday as forty-eight countries from across the world voted in favour of a new set of global human rights.

According to its original foundation charter, the United Nations was created to encourage a "universal respect for, and observance of, human rights and fundamental freedoms for all without distinction as to race, sex, language, or religion". However, after the atrocities of the Second World War many have questioned whether the UN has done enough to try to protect these rights.

The new charter, called the Universal Declaration of Human Rights, goes into more detail as to what these human rights are, as well as making clear that all countries should be expected to respect them. It calls them "a common standard of achievement for all peoples and all nations".

The Declaration has been drafted over two years by 18 committee members from various countries and political persuasions in a bid to lay out an unbiased set of fundamental rights.

Heading the committee is Eleanor Roosevelt, well known across the globe for her advocacy for human rights. In a speech yesterday in Paris, she said the Declaration "may well become the international Magna Carta of all men everywhere", a reference to the English charter which represents a cornerstone document on the road to universal rights and liberty.

The UN Declaration did not get universal support, however. Of the eight countries which abstained from voting, not voting either yes or no, six were countries in the Soviet Union's sphere of influence.

It has been suggested this was because of the inclusion in the Declaration of the right of an individual to leave a country and live elsewhere. It is thought the Soviet authorities were worried this could provoke a mass exodus to the West. Also abstaining were Saudi Arabia and South Africa, owing to its racial apartheid policy.

It's legal to be gay at last!

By our home affairs editor, July 28, 1967

CENTURIES of legal tradition that treated homosexuals as criminals have been abandoned in a triumphant parliamentary result for homosexual-rights activists in the UK.

The debate over the changes, which are still unpopular with much of the population, carried on well into the night. The legislation does not yet grant total equality between homo- and heterosexuals, but does decriminalise homosexuality in certain situations.

Furthermore, the Act does not apply to Scotland and Northern Ireland, where homosexual acts are still illegal and punished with harsh sentences.

Over the last few decades, the British government has strictly enforced laws against male homosexuality, putting thousands of gay men in prisons, often at a young age, for the 'offence'. Meanwhile, it has never been an offence for women to be gay.

One well-known victim of maltreatment for being a male homosexual was the famous wartime codebreaker Alan Turing. It was thanks to his revolutionary genius that British agents managed to crack the Nazi 'Enigma code' during the Second World War. His achievements made an incalculable contribution to the war effort and computer technology.

Turing was tried as a homosexual in 1952, and chose to undergo hormone therapy instead of prison. The therapy made him infertile. He was found dead two years later. It is widely thought his suicide was linked to the treatment he was given.

CIVIL RIGHTS ACT FINALLY MAKES ALL MEN EQUAL IN EYES OF THE LAW

By our US Bureau, July 2, 1964

MARTIN LUTHER KING'S dream may at last be coming true as the USA signs into law an historic Civil Rights Act outlawing all forms of discrimination based on race, colour, religion, sex or national origin.

Prior to the new law, many states had implemented a policy of segregation, especially racial segregation against black people, with schools, workplaces, parks, lifts, public facilities and the vote all being targets for discrimination. Black Americans, including children, have also faced violence and abuse across the country from groups such as the Ku Klux Klan and the police.

Today's success can be put down to the powerful movement to end the racial segregation against black Americans which has been ongoing for generations despite the ban on slavery almost exactly 100 years ago.

The Civil Rights Movement first grabbed the headlines in 1955 when Rosa Parks, a seamstress from Alabama, was arrested for refusing to give up her seat on a bus to a white man.

Amongst the subsequent bus boycott's leaders was Martin Luther King, a local pastor and now national icon for change, whose march on Washington DC last year brought an estimated 250,000 civil rights supporters to the capital.

King's impromptu "I Have a Dream" speech, in which he called upon America to uphold its creed that "all men are created equal", is now being hailed as one of the greatest speeches of all time.

As Iron Curtain falls, hopes rise for new freedoms across Europe

Gorbachev's 'glasnost' may lead to the collapse of the Soviet Union

By our Berlin correspondent, November 10, 1989

THE GREAT WALL dividing the historic capital of united Germany between East and West has finally fallen. For the first time in more than a generation Berliners yesterday joined each other in euphoric celebration on either side of their city.

As East and West Berliners are reunited, after years of entrapment, people dubbed 'Wall Woodpeckers' have been seen chipping off parts of the Wall to save as souvenirs!

The Berlin Wall emerged in 1961 as barbed wire and barriers blocked the border, preventing East and West Berliners from crossing into each other's halves of the city. From that moment on, families and friends were divided for decades. The Wall was later constructed as a concrete barrier complete with minefields and guards ready to shoot and kill anyone trying to cross.

Following the Second World War Germany was split into two states, East and West. The Communist East was controlled by the Soviet Union, while the capitalist West comprised nations that were supported by the USA. These two factions then engaged in a decades-long 'Cold War', so called because direct conflict never took place.

Commentators believe that the fall of the Berlin Wall – dubbed the 'Iron Curtain' by UK wartime premier Winston Churchill in March 1946 – may mark the end of an ideologically divided Europe.

Discontent in the Communist East has been brewing for nearly a decade following strikes in Poland by the Communist world's first unofficial trade union, Solidarity, headed by Lech Wałęsa.

Apartheid ends: de Klerk and Mandela agree terms

By our South Africa correspondent, November 19, 1993

RACIAL INJUSTICE in South Africa may at last be nearing an end as the government yesterday gave in to demands for its first-ever multiracial general election.

The announcement follows successful negotiations between Nelson Mandela, who was imprisoned for 27 years, and President de Klerk.

The election will end the decades-old system of enforced segregation between people of different races in the country – known as apartheid, Afrikaans for 'apartness'.

Apartheid has seen blacks and other races denied basic rights such as voting, free speech and living in white areas. The policy has resulted in an ever-increasing spiral of racial violence and large-scale poverty along racial lines.

Mandela's party, called the African National Congress (ANC), has the support of the majority of now-enfranchised black voters. It is expected to win the election and Mandela himself may soon become the country's first black president.

UN *urged to give rights to all Apes*

A GROUP OF ANIMAL RIGHTS activists has launched a campaign for great apes to be given some of the same basic rights as humans, writes our UN correspondent.

The Great Ape Project has been set up by a group of philosophers and scientists and is pushing for a UN declaration of rights for chimpanzees, bonobos, gorillas and orangutans.

Supporters, such as the primatologist Jane Goodall, argue that since Great Apes share many similarities with humans in regard to their social and emotional lives they should be entitled to similar rights.

So far, the group is campaigning for the UN to recognise the Great Ape's Right to Life and to protect them from torture and unlawful incarceration – which would mean any 'non-criminal' apes in zoos and medical labs throughout the world would have to be released.

Schism threatened as Church of England votes in favour of the ordination of women priests

By our religious affairs correspondent,
November 12, 1992

AN HISTORIC VOTE was passed last night by the smallest of margins allowing women to be ordained as priests. It follows long discussions by the General Synod, the Church of England's parliament.

The new law means women will be ordained. This will allow them to celebrate Communion, a significant ritual within Anglicanism, bringing the ancient established Church closer towards full equality between the genders.

Despite the vote, a significant number of priests and parishioners have threatened to resign or leave the Anglican Church over the changes.

Opponents of the new law claim that the Synod has placed liberty and equality above sacred scriptures and religious texts which, they claim, reserve the priesthood as a males-only office. Lay people outside the Church have also spoken out against the ruling, many of whom are considering converting to the more orthodox Roman Catholicism.

Aware of the disagreement, George Carey, Archbishop of Canterbury, called for unity, saying: "What binds us together in God's love as a Church is vastly more important than a disagreement about women's ordination."

Currently, 1,400 Church of England women are waiting to be ordained as priests. Even so, the fight for full equality isn't over yet. Those campaigning for women to have a greater role in the Church are now looking to the future for a first female bishop in England, an office still reserved for men.

Human Rights Act passes in UK

SUPPORT FOR human rights received parliamentary affirmation last night as a new Act was passed which will speed up the process of bringing human rights abusers to justice, writes our Westminster reporter, November 10, 1998.

Although the UK has been a signatory to the European Convention on Human Rights for almost 50 years, bringing cases to the European Court is a lengthy process which can take five years and cost up to £30,000. The new Act will unite European law with UK law and allow human rights trials to take place more quickly and easily in the UK, rather than having to be taken all the way to Strasbourg in France.

The law will also make it easier to prosecute powerful groups, including politicians, who show too little respect for human rights laws. It also outlaws the death penalty in the UK, which was last given as a sentence in 1964, leading to the hanging of two men. Until now, death by hanging has been technically available as a punishment but only in certain military situations.

Bhutto killed on election trail

By our Pakistan correspondent,
December 28, 2007

THE IRON LADY of Pakistan, former prime minister Benazir Bhutto, was assassinated yesterday while campaigning against the current government during the run-up to the next Pakistani general election.

The killing will send shock waves throughout the world. As the first-ever female leader of a Muslim country Mrs Bhutto represented the face of modernity in the hearts and minds of many Pakistani people. She championed democratic and egalitarian values within an otherwise deeply conservative state.

Benazir Bhutto was the eldest child of former Pakistani prime minister Zulfikar Ali Bhutto, founder of the Pakistan People's Party (PPP).

Mrs Bhutto became leader of the PPP just three years after her father's execution in 1979, becoming a celebrity role model for aspiring women in Muslim countries keen to involve themselves in politics.

But Bhutto's trailblazing rise to prominence caused substantial resentment amongst conservative Muslims. She eventually became prime minister in 1988, but her government was engulfed by scandals following an economic downturn. In 1993 she won a second term in office and survived an attempted military coup two years later. It was during these years that her tough line against trade unions earned her the title the Iron Lady – echoing the name given to Britain's first female prime minister, Margaret Thatcher.

Corruption charges in 1996 led to the fall of Bhutto's second administration. However, following a formal acquittal of all charges against her earlier this year, she returned from exile to participate in fresh elections with the aim of re-entering front-line Pakistani politics for a third time.

Her assassination yesterday comes as a body blow for people who want to see a more prominent role for women in Muslim society.

Press freedoms should be regulated in law says phone-hacking inquiry

By our media editor, London, November 30, 2012

LORD JUSTICE LEVESON has released his report on intrusions into personal privacy by the press, broadcasters and social media after a public inquiry that has taken more than 16 months to complete.

Allegations of privacy intrusions surfaced in 2011 after it was revealed that in 2002 *News of the World* reporters and private investigators hacked into the voicemail of the then-missing-teenager Milly Dowler. She was later found to have been abducted and murdered. It has now been revealed that the paper had been spying on many other individuals, including celebrities and the Royal Family, in a bid to gain exclusive stories.

The Prime Minister called for a full investigation into breaches of privacy and the dubious practices that papers and some journalists were using to find information. Police investigations have so far led to the arrest of several journalists. Meanwhile, groups such as 'Hacked Off', who were instrumental in bringing about the investigation, have been campaigning for stricter rules to govern the press.

Leveson's report calls for a new body to regulate the press with guarantees of its impartiality enshrined in statute. Some are saying the suggestions are not strict enough, while others, especially the papers, are resisting the changes.

Representatives of the press say the new laws contravene centuries-old traditions protecting freedom of expression and free speech.

Snowden seeks end to state snooping

By our Asia staff, Hong Kong, June 10, 2013

AMERICAN COMPUTER whizz Edward Snowden was yesterday identified as the anonymous whistleblower who only five days ago is alleged to have leaked a cache of secret documents. They are said to reveal a huge spying operation that is being carried out in secret by America and its allies against ordinary civilians.

Snowden's documents propose that everything, from the private mobile phone calls of heads of state, including allies such as the German chancellor Angela Merkel, to the emails and social media messages of people across the globe, is routinely targeted by Western state-run mass surveillance operations.

According to Snowden no one has been overlooked by America's global intelligence agency, the NSA, or Britain's spy agency, GCHQ, with even charities being secretly watched.

Commentators believe that Snowden, who has worked as a contractor for various intelligence agencies, including the NSA, will soon be amongst the most wanted men in the world for revealing such intimate state secrets.

. Yesterday, during an interview held in a Hong Kong hotel, Snowden explained his actions, saying he wanted a frank, open debate to be held to discuss the right balance between the needs of national security and hard-won civil rights designed to safeguard individual liberty and privacy.

Snowden claimed such a discussion has been denied democratic scrutiny owing to an overzealous state reaction to the so-called 'War on Terror'.

Gay couples are made legally equivalent in British law

By our religious editor, July 18, 2013

England and Wales will legally recognise same-sex marriages, according to a new law passed yesterday in Parliament. A similar bill has already been introduced to the Scottish Parliament.

Same-sex couples have been entitled to 'civil partnerships' since 2004. However they are not offered all of the same legal rights as married couples and the government has previously insisted they cannot be described as 'married'. Also, the use of religious symbols, texts or music has been prohibited at civil partnership ceremonies.

Many same-sex couples argue these differences show they are not treated equally, an injustice which undermines a fundamental human right to choose your own partner, regardless of background, age or sex.

But thanks to yesterday's vote same-sex couples can now plan for equal marriage under the law.

A number of couples are already vying to claim the title of first-ever married same-sex couple by planning their weddings as close as possible to March 13 next year when the new law comes into force.

However, to the dismay of many, Anglican priests are still officially banned from marrying gay couples in church.

Women take to cars in protest at controversial ban on driving

CAMPAIGNERS took to the roads in Riyadh, Saudi Arabia, yesterday to protest against a nationwide ban on female drivers, writes our Middle East correspondent, October 27, 2013.

More than 17,000 people have signed a petition calling for women to be allowed to drive or for a full explanation to be given as to why the ban should remain in force.

Yesterday's protest was the third since 1990, when nearly four dozen women drove around the city for half an hour until they were arrested by police. The ban is informal rather than enshrined in Sharia law.

Saudi Arabia is the only country in the world where women are not allowed to hold a driving licence. Women's rights in Saudi Arabia generally are more restricted than in the West: women cannot vote, they must have a male guardian and must wear the hijab, a veil to cover the head, in public. Such limitations have their roots in a strict interpretation

of Sunni Islam, the official state religion.

The campaign to allow women to drive cars has been denounced in mosques across the country as being bent on destroying traditional Saudi society.

But to some Saudi women, driving is a matter of personal liberty, allowing them to travel independently across the vast country to places of education and work without having to pay for a man to act as a chauffeur.

Arab Spring turns to Arab Winter as anarchy and terrorism sweep in

Attempts to foster freedom in Middle East flail and falter

By our Middle East editor, Damascus, December 17, 2013

THEY WERE INTOXICATED by dreams of liberty and freedom. But now the lives of protestors across the Middle East, whose popular resistance that began three years ago became known as the Arab Spring, are being ripped apart by wars, terrorism and religious fundamentalism which have cost the lives of millions.

The desperate plight of people stretching from Libya to Syria, via Egypt and Somalia, has its origins in a series of protests which began in Tunisia three years ago today when a fruit and vegetable seller named Mohamed Bouazizi, from a quiet town in Tunisia, literally took his life into his own hands after arguing with local police.

When Bouazizi's scales were confiscated by an officious police officer, the street trader covered himself in gasoline and set himself on fire in front of the local governor's office. It was a desperate act of defiance and protest at being unable to work and feed his family.

That single tragic act lit the touchpaper on a groundswell of popular discontent, sparking waves of spontaneous protests which quickly spilled out into surrounding regions.

Unemployment, low pay, state surveillance, police brutality and the dictatorial rule of President Zine El Abidine Ben Ali, who had been in power for 23 years, were the focus of the people's discontent.

Three years on and Tunisia seems to have emerged on a path towards democracy and greater personal freedoms.

But neighbouring countries, whose people were inspired by events in Tunisia, have seen their worlds turned upside down.

Many commentators are saying that what began as an 'Arab Spring' in pursuit of individual freedoms and liberties has now turned into a terrible 'Arab Winter', imperilling the lives of countless millions.

In Syria tens of thousands of children have been orphaned in a civil war between autocratic President Assad and the popular opposition, split between pro Western democrats and Islamic fundamentalist 'freedom fighters'.

Protests in Egypt against the long-time dictator Hosni Mubarak had looked set to usher in a new period of democracy, but then a military coup ousting the freely elected president Mohamed Morsi in July this year has led to the return of military rule.

In Libya, international military intervention, led by Britain and France, helped rebels overthrow the country's dictator Muammar Gaddafi. But today Libya is ruled by rival groups and commentators fear that, like Syria, the country could soon descend into being run by gangs or flip into outright civil war.

Royal and Ancient golfers finally accept women

SCOTLAND'S PEOPLE may have decided not to end three centuries of union, but St Andrews' golf club – dubbed the home of golf – yesterday voted to break with 260 years of tradition and accept women into its fold, writes our golf correspondent, September 19, 2014.

The change follows calls from ex-prime minister Gordon Brown for the club to abandon its male-only traditions.

St Andrews acts as the governing body for the sport outside the USA and Mexico, and therefore makes important decisions regarding rules and regulations, as well as organising many of the major competitions worldwide, including the highly prestigious Open Championship.

Yesterday's vote means women as well as men will be able to determine the future rules and regulations of this globally popular sport.

Scots reject independence in giant turnout

By our Scotland editor, Edinburgh, September 19, 2014

THE WAITING is finally over. Yesterday the people of Scotland made their feelings on independence clear by voting decisively against leaving the United Kingdom.

The historic vote means Scotland will continue to stand united as part of Great Britain. However, with whole cities such as Glasgow voting with a majority in favour of independence, politicians will nevertheless look anxiously at the astounding support for national freedom generated during the campaign.

Alex Salmond, leader of the independence movement and First Minister of Scotland, said that, despite the undesired result, the referendum was a "triumph for the democratic process and for participation in politics".

The referendum, in which individuals aged 16 and over were entitled to vote directly for or against independence rather than through elected representatives to Parliament, achieved the massive turnout of 85 per cent of the Scottish electorate.

The power of this democratic process for enabling the public themselves to answer such a crucial question was praised by major figures both in the UK and across the globe, including US President Barack Obama who described it as a "full and energetic exercise of democracy".

Other independence movements across the world have taken note of the huge potential in referenda for democratic representation. Principal figures in the Basque and Catalonian independence movements in Spain have described the referendum as a model democratic process they hope to see utilised within their own regions.

Although support for independence is perhaps even stronger in these regions, the Spanish government has repeatedly said that it would block separation. Some believe that Catalonia and the Basque Country's increasing desire for independence may be dead in the water if the currently unsympathetic Spanish administration ignores the democratic will of its regions and denies them a proper vote.

Internet pioneer Berners-Lee calls for new 'Magna Carta' to protect the Internet

Liberties are being eroded by government snooping says Web inventor

By our media correspondent, London, March 13, 2014,

THE INVENTOR of the World Wide Web, Sir Tim Berners-Lee, has spoken out against government and corporate control of the Internet. A global "Bill of Rights" to preserve the Internet as a free and independent tool, usable by anyone, is now essential, he has suggested.

Berners-Lee said that powerful groups were exercising increasing control over the Internet solely for their own benefit, such as in the extensive surveillance operations recently brought to light by whistleblower Edward Snowden.

A neutral Internet without the influence of governments or organisations is essential to supporting "open government, good democracy, good healthcare, connected communities and the diversity of culture", he said.

Berners-Lee said people are losing sight of these objectives: "Our rights are being infringed more and more on every side, and the danger is that we get used to it."

Making references to the fundamental English legal text Magna Carta, Berners-Lee called on the world to produce its own 'digital Bill of Rights' which would enshrine areas of the Internet and particular freedoms as out of bounds to governments and corporations.

Berners-Lee argues that since the Internet can be used by anyone for communicating information to the wider world, it is an essential medium for freedom of speech and democracy. This freedom is what Berners-Lee suggests is now being eroded by spooks who take advantage of it to spy on citizens and silence debate.

Berners-Lee began developing his concept of the World Wide Web whilst working at CERN, the largest particle physics laboratory in the world, at the time a centre for Internet research. The Web's first website was published in 1991.

Ever since, he has worked internationally to make the World Wide Web a global tool for spreading information freely. He has also helped to make the Internet available in countries where most people have no access.

Celebrating right to be educated: Malala wins Nobel Peace Prize

THE NOBEL PEACE PRIZE, the world's most prestigious award given to those who further international peace, was yesterday awarded to Malala Yousafzai, the youngest person ever to receive the accolade, *writes our Norway correspondent, October 11, 2014.*

Malala, aged 17, was chosen to receive the award for campaigning in Pakistan and the rest of the world in support of the right of all children to have an education.

Two years ago Malala was shot in the head while on her way to school by religious radicals in Pakistan who say it is not appropriate for girls to have an education. She fell into a coma but narrowly survived after receiving intensive treatment for her injuries at the Queen Elizabeth Hospital in Birmingham, England.

Since then Malala has been a vociferous campaigner for the right of all females to go to school, regardless of their background, social status, colour or creed.

Malala has been campaigning on education issues in Pakistan for the BBC since the age of 11 under the pseudonym 'Gul Makai', a local folklore heroine. Occupation by the Taliban, a religious extremist group, in the region where she lives

LIVE Oslo

HAPPENING NOW
NOBEL PEACE PRIZE AWARDED TO MALALA YOUSAFZAI

led to the widespread suppression of education for girls. Despite the repeated closure of schools by the Taliban and their increasing fury at her outspoken beliefs, Malala continued going to school and publishing her reports.

In October 2012 a Taliban gunman shot Malala on a school bus. Two of her classmates were also injured in the attack.

Malala was soon campaigning again for education and communicating worldwide with other young education activists. Celebrating her 16th birthday by speaking before the United Nations and over 500 young education activists, she gave her support to "every woman, every boy and every girl who have raised their voice for their rights".

The world should "pick up our books and our pens", she said, since "they are our most powerful weapons". Malala argued that education gives children the best possible opportunity to free themselves from poverty and exploitation in later life.

While many Pakistanis have expressed support for her views, radical elements still have a lot of influence. The nation currently ranks amongst the lowest for its support for girls' education. Malala hopes that some day soon every child will have access to schools in a safe environment.

Crowds gather to mark 800 years in the fight for freedom and rights

By our home affairs correspondent, Runnymede, Windsor, June 16, 2015

THOUSANDS of people gathered yesterday in the water meadow at Runnymede to commemorate the 800th anniversary of the sealing of Magna Carta by unpopular King John who was famously forced into agreeing to limit his royal powers by a gang of rebellious barons.

This single act – widely remembered as the first effort to limit the divine right of kings to do as they please – has now become the pivot around which evolved the story of how absolute power in the feudal age eventually gave way to democracy in over 100 countries throughout the world today.

Personal freedoms such as the right to free speech, a fair trial, political representation and peaceful protest were yesterday celebrated as having begun 800 years ago after the English barony

grew tired of having their wealth taxed by the King for his failed French wars without first being asked for their approval.

Since then myriad threads, ranging from the freedom of nations to choose their governments to gender and race equality, have

become woven into a global drive towards the recognition of universal human rights.

Yesterday the Magna Carta memorial at Runnymede was rededicated by members of the Royal Family and the Magna Carta Trust, a body formed to perpetuate

the principles of Magna Carta shortly after the inauguration of the memorial itself in 1957.

Stephen Zack, trustee and former president of the American Bar Association, said the importance of this year's commemorations was impossible to overstate.

"This represents the single best opportunity in our lifetime to educate people about the importance of the rule of law," he said.

Sir Robert Worcester, deputy chairman of the Magna Carta Trust and chairman of the Magna Carta 800th Committee, the body co-ordinating this year's worldwide commemorations, warned that the fight for freedoms is far from over.

"Freedoms are being eroded faster than they can be won. That's why it is vital to take the time to step back and look with wonder at what has been achieved over the last 800 years," he said.

The Chronicle Crossword

Across

3. First female leader of a Muslim country
5. A seasonal change in the Middle East
6. Jack Cade's bête noire
8. Pope who excommunicated King John
10. Middle East country torn apart by civil war
11. Italian city appoints first female professor
13. Spanish dictator
15. Gutenberg's profession
20. Significance of the third suffragette colour
21. The Parliament Act's personal champion
23. French home town of J. S. Mill
24. Papal list of forbidden books
26. _____ only allowed in, until recently
29. The Black Death's continent of origin
30. Judge who led inquiry over press freedoms
32. Computer whizz given hormone therapy
34. Name given to first American colony
35. Man who brought printing press to England
37. First name of notoriously rebellious baron
38. Mammal victim of a cruel fruit seller
39. Constituency home of first resident female MP
40. What Martin Luther King said he had
41. English lawyer who helped draft 1618 charter

Down

1. Sport played at Royal & Ancient
2. US Founding Father
3. Once taxed in Russia
4. Delegates met here in the Woods
5. Dutch leader who helped usurp James II
7. Confiscated from a Tunisian tradesman
9. Alfred _____, creator of peace prize
12. French revolutionaries' killing machine
13. Courageous Maid's country of origin
14. Medieval religious dissident
16. Place where American spy explained all
17. South American freedom fighter
18. _____ Tyler, as a homophone
19. Dangled in front of Tip O'Neill
22. Heliocentric heretic
23. Indian king fond of edicts
25. Roman slave leader
27. Charter to be overseen by 25 _____
28. Honour refused by T. E. Lawrence
30. Place where Henry III was captured
31. Inspirational wife of J. S. Mill
33. Goddess of Bedloe Island
36. French city where Wars of Religion ended
37. First appeared in *The Harrisburg Pennsylvanian*, although that's a matter of opinion

All the correct answers can be found somewhere inside the book or on the timeline overleaf

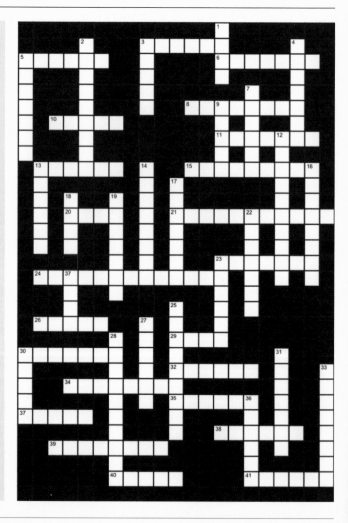

THE MAGNA CARTA CHRONICLE Quiz

Try this amazing 50-question quiz to test out your knowledge of key moments in the struggle for freedom and liberties over 800 years.

The correct answers can be found somewhere inside this book or on the timeline overleaf.

1. Which ancient ruler was responsible for creating the oldest surviving legal code?
   a) Alexander the Great
   b) Nebuchadnezzar
   c) Cyrus the Great
   d) Hammurabi

2. The Cyrus Cylinder was discovered in the ruins of which ancient city?
   a) Babylon
   b) Troy
   c) Persepolis
   d) Aleppo

3. Which Roman general finally defeated the army of rebel slave leader Spartacus?
   a) Caesar
   b) Crassus
   c) Pompey
   d) Cicero

4. Which Anglo-Saxon king created England's first codified set of laws?
   a) Aethelred
   b) Aethelberht
   c) Aethelstan
   d) Eggnog

5. How many barons were charged with overseeing that Magna Carta was adhered to by the King?
   a) 10
   b) 12
   c) 20
   d) 25

6. Which of the following cities was NOT sent a copy of Magna Carta?
   a) Durham
   b) Salisbury
   c) Hereford
   d) Milton Keynes

7. In 1264 Simon de Montfort captured King Henry III at the Battle of
   a) Evesham
   b) Lewes
   c) Bosworth Field
   d) Blenheim

8. Which creatures spread the Black Death to humans in Europe and devastated the continent?
   a) Mice
   b) Bats
   c) Squirrels
   d) Fleas

9. Sumptuary laws are designed to do what?
   a) Determine the quality of cloth worn by peasants
   b) Promote the sale of exclusive fabrics
   c) Help prevent the spread of TB
   d) Encourage people to improve their maths

10. Which preacher stirred up peasants into revolt alongside Wat Tyler in 1381?
    a) John Smith
    b) John Ball
    c) John Brown
    d) John Best

11. In Shakespeare's play *Henry VI, Part 2*, peasant leader Jack Cade and his cohorts agree that the first thing they will do during their rebellion is
    a) Go to the pub
    b) Kill all the lawyers
    c) Burn London Bridge
    d) Pay penance

12. Which of the following machines inspired Johannes Gutenberg when he was making his first moveable-type printing press?
    a) A flower press
    b) A wine press
    c) An olive press
    d) A trouser press

ELEANOR ROOSEVELT
Human rights campaigner

MARTIN LUTHER KING
Civil rights campaigner

MIKHAIL GORBACHEV
Communist reformer

MAGNA EXCHANGE
-1942-

WINSTON CHURCHILL tries to force Lincoln Cathedral to donate its copy of Magna Carta to the United States government as a gift to thank them for supporting Britain and its allies in the Second World War. It did go to America – and was safeguarded at Fort Knox – but was returned to Lincoln after the war was over

EUROPEAN CONVENTION
-1950-

A CONVENTION guaranteeing human rights is passed into European law. It is not adopted by the UK until 1998 with the Human Rights Act

FOUR BASIC FREEDOMS
-1941-

FRANKLIN ROOSEVELT'S State of the Union address to the US Congress outlines four basic freedoms: the freedom of speech and religion and the freedom from want and fear

FREE TRADE
-1944-

ECONOMISTS from Western nations meet in the US state of New Hampshire at Bretton Woods and establish a system of free trading between nations underpinned by national central banks

UNITED NATIONS
-1948-

THE UNITED NATIONS Universal Declaration of Human Rights is passed by the UN with 48 votes in favour and 8 abstentions (including South Africa and Saudi Arabia). Eleanor Roosevelt declares it "may well become the international Magna Carta of all men everywhere"

I'M GAY AND IT'S OK
-1967-

HOMOSEXUALITY is decriminalised in England and Wales for people aged 21 and over after Parliament passes the Sexual Offences Act. Scotland follows in 1980 and Northern Ireland in 1982. The age of consent is lowered to 16, in line with hetero-sexuals, in the year 2000

ALP LAST
-1971-

SWITZERLAND is one of the last Western European nations to grant women the right to vote in parliamentary elections, with some cantons not extending the franchise until 1991

VOTING RIGHTS ACT
-1965-

AFRICAN AMERICANS are finally granted proper voting rights following the Civil Rights Movement led by Martin Luther King

OVERSEAS VOTING RIGHTS
-1975-

TEA BAGS are dangled in front of Tip O'Neill in the House of Representatives by overseas Americans demanding either quitting having to pay US income tax or getting the right to vote in federal elections. President Ford signs the Overseas Citizens Voting Rights Act into law the following year

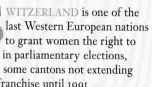

SPANISH SPRING
-1977-

FREE VOTING in elections resumes in Spain after a gap of 41 years dominated by the dictatorship of Francisco Franco

MARGARET THATCHER
1979 - 1990

BRITAIN ELECTS its first and, so far, only female prime minister

WO
PR

THE EN Ge approves th women as narrow ma

IRON CURTAIN FALLS
-1989-

A CONCRETE WALL dividing Europe is demolished. It follows a policy of openness pursued by the last Soviet leader Mikhail Gorbachev

MONKEY BUSINESS
-1994-

AN INTERNATIONAL CA based in Brazil is launche persuade the United Nat basic legal rights to non-human It is called the Great Ape Proje

SOUTH AFRICAN FREEDOM
1994 - 1999

NELSON MANDELA, a black South African anti-apartheid activist, who spent 27 years in jail for his efforts to have liberties granted to black South Africans, becomes the president of South Africa

JUNE 4th PROTESTS
-1989-

CHINESE STUDENTS gather in Tiananmen Squ in a bid to secure the right to vote in free elect Protesters are gunned down by the military. E of the numbers killed range from a few hundred to se

94   1960   1980

NELSON MANDELA
First black president of South Africa

BENAZIR BHUTTO
First female prime minister of Pakistan

MALALA YOUSAFZAI
Educational rights campaigner

...MEN ...ESTS
- ...92 -

...CHURCH OF ...LAND'S ...eral Synod ... ordination of ...iests by a ...gin

LOVE IS...
- 2013 -

SAME SEX MARRIAGES give gay couples the same legal status as marriage does for heterosexuals in the UK

SCOTTISH REFERENDUM
- 2014 -

SCOTTISH PEOPLE vote not to secede from the UK after a record voter turnout. Despite a defeat for independence, clamour grows for a more federalised UK

LADIES AT LAST
- 2014 -

THE ROYAL & ANCIENT GOLF CLUB OF ST ANDREWS finally admits women members for the first time in its 260-year history

INTERNET MAGNA CARTA
- 2014 -

TIM BERNERS-LEE, the British inventor of the World Wide Web, calls for a new Magna Carta of the Web to ensure personal liberties are free from state interference

MAGNA CARTA 800th
- 2015 -

COMMEMORATIONS are held throughout the world on the 800th anniversary of Magna Carta to acknowledge its principles as the foundation stone of modern democracy, the rule of law and human rights

...MPAIGN,
...d to try to ...ions to grant ...great apes. ...t

STATE SNOOPING UNMASKED
- 2013 -

AMERICAN COMPUTER professional Edward Snowden leaks secret US and UK government files showing mass surveillance of telecommunications and the Internet, including the tapping of German Chancellor Angela Merkel's mobile phone. Fierce debates follow on the right balance between personal privacy and national security

ARAB SPRING
2010 - 2014

FRUIT SELLER Mohamed Bouazizi from Tunisia sets himself on fire in protest after his scales are confiscated by officials. His sacrifice triggers a wave of protests demanding greater freedoms and rights for people living in Muslim countries

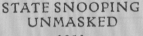

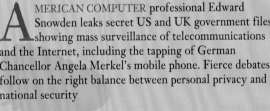

Elizabeth R 2013

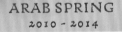

BENAZIR BHUTTO - RIP
- 2007 -

THE FIRST-EVER female prime minister of a Muslim country is assassinated whilst on the campaign trail

...are, Beijing, ...ions. ...stimates ...veral thousand

COMMONWEALTH CHARTER
- 2013 -

A CHARTER setting out the values of the Commonwealth is signed by Elizabeth II on 11th March 2013. It contains 16 core rights and beliefs

NOBEL PEACE PRIZE
- 2014 -

MALALA YOUSAFZAI, a Pakistani teenager shot by extremists for going to school, is awarded the Nobel Peace Prize

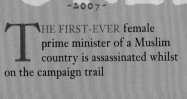

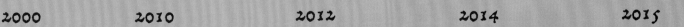

2000   2010   2012   2014   2015

THE SALISBURY CATHEDRAL
MAGNA CARTA

THE SALISBURY CATHEDRAL Magna Carta is one of at least 13 copies that were issued in 1215. It is the finest of the four surviving originals, thanks to the good condition of the parchment and the quality of the writing, crisp even under high magnification. Some of Magna Carta's key clauses, which are still relevant in laws today, are explained below:

FREEDOM OF THE CHURCH
(Clause 1)

FIRST, THAT WE HAVE granted to God, and by this present charter have confirmed for us and our heirs in perpetuity, that the English Church shall be free, and shall have its rights undiminished, and its liberties unimpaired.

NO TAXATION WITHOUT
REPRESENTATION
(Clause 12)

NO 'SCUTAGE' or 'aid' may be levied in our kingdom without its general consent, unless it is for the ransom of our person, to make our eldest son a knight, and (once) to marry our eldest daughter. For these purposes only a reasonable 'aid' may be levied. 'Aids' from the city of London are to be treated similarly.

LAURA BASSI
Professor

THOMAS JEFFERSON
Founding Father

WILLIAM WILBERFORCE
Parliamentarian

FREE TRADE
- 1776 -

SCOTTISH ECONOMIST Adam Smith proposes a system of free trade and market forces to improve the wealth of nations

LIBERTÉ, ÉGALITÉ, FRATERNITÉ,
1789 - 1799

FRENCH REVOLUTIONARIES declare the rights of man and the citizens. Its leaders embark on an orgy of violence, targeting the monarchy and aristocracy. France grants universal suffrage to all men in 1792 and abolishes slavery two years later, although it is reinstated by Napoleon in 1802

THE RIGHTS OF MAN
-1776 -

THE PREAMBLE to the US Declaration of Independence, drafted by Founding Father Thomas Jefferson, establishes the inalienable right of all men to life, liberty and the pursuit of happiness

BOSTON TEA PARTY
- 1773 -

AMERICAN COLONISTS, disguised as Native Americans, dump tea in Boston Harbor in protest at 'no taxation without representation'

FIRST FEMALE PROFESSOR
- 1732 -

LAURA BASSI, an Italian scientist, becomes the first woman to earn a professional teaching position at a European university, in Bologna, Italy

REFORM BILLS & RIS
1832

THE UK PARLIAMENT passes 1832 which increases the vot males, grants new seats to la 'rotten boroughs'. But it is not enoug petitions in a movement known as C of 1867 further extends voting rights

SLAVERY BANNED
-1833 -

FOLLOWING A LIFELONG camp by William Wilberforce, owning slaves becomes illegal throughou the British Empire

TRIAL OF BILL BURNS
- 1822 -

A JUDGE IN LONDON fines a fruit seller for being cruel to a donkey. It is the first-ever prosecution under an Act prohibiting the improper treatment of horses and cattle, championed by Colonel Richard Martin

OPINION POLL
-1824 -

A US NEWSPAPER, *The Harrisburg Pennsylvanian*, publishes the first opinion poll, showing Andrew Jackson leading the race to become US president

SOUTH AMERICAN FREEDOM
1808 - 1833

FOLLOWING A FRENCH invasion of Spain, colonies in South America make a bid for independence from European rule. Venezuelan leader Simón Bolívar frees Venezuela, Colombia, Ecuador, Peru and Bolivia

HAITIAN INDEPENDENCE
1791 - 1804

SLAVES REBEL in the French colony of St Domingue leading to the founding of the Republic of Haiti. Rebel leader Jean-Jacques Dessalines is chosen as the country's founding father

ABRAHAM LINCOLN
16th president of The United States

T.E. LAWRENCE
Freedom fighter

EMMELINE PANKHURST
Suffragette

OF THE CHARTISTS
-1867-

The Great Reform Act in
ng franchise to 1 in 5 adult
ge towns and abolishes
. Millions of people sign
artism. The Reform Act
to more men

aign

OFF TO SCHOOL
-1870-

COMPULSORY EDUCATION begins in Britain for all children aged between five and 13, at school 'or otherwise'

ON LIBERTY
-1859-

BRITISH PHILOSOPHER John Stuart Mill argues that state control should be limited. His book becomes a cornerstone of free-market capitalism

TRADE UNIONS
-1899-

THE GENERAL FEDERATION of Trade Unions is formed in Britain. Its objective is to support unions demanding better pay and conditions

UNIVERSAL SUFFRAG
-1928-

WOMEN are granted the same voting rights as men across the United Kingdom

SUFFRAGETTES
-1911-

WOMEN LIBERALS in the UK protest over not being given the right to vote. In 1913 suffragette Emily Davison tries to pin a 'Votes for Women' banner on to the King's horse at the Epsom races, but is trampled to death

CIVIL WAR
1861-1865

AFTER A BITTER civil war the USA finally bans slavery. The 14th Amendment, passed in 1868, grants former slaves the right to vote but many states mount legal challenges

STATUE OF LIBERTY
-1886-

THE FRENCH PEOPLE give a statue of the Roman goddess Libertas to the citizens of the United States. It is erected in New York Harbor as a welcoming icon for immigrants arriving from persecution abroad

PARLIAMENT ACT
-1911-

IT IS ESTABLISHED by law in Westminster that elected members of the House of Commons are the supreme lawmakers, removing the veto powers of the aristocracy

THE 19th AMENDMENT
-1920-

VOTING RIGHTS are extended to women in the USA, 42 years after the measure was first introduced into the House of Congress

JAPANESE REFORMS
-1875-

YUKICHI FUKUZAWA writes *An Outline of a Theory of Civilisation* in which he argues that personal freedom is achieved through education. His newspaper, *Jiji Shimpo*, promotes liberalisation and reform in Japan

UNIVERSAL SUFFRAGE
1893

NEW ZEALAND becomes the first country in the world to grant universal suffrage (extending voting rights to women as well as men)

LAWRENCE OF ARABIA
1916-1918

DESPITE HIS BEST efforts, British army officer T.E. Lawrence fails to persuade British and French officials to grant Arab states political freedom and independence. Following the end of World War I, Lawrence is offered a Victoria Cross and a knighthood but refuses both

OFFICIAL BALLOT
PRESIDENTIAL ELECTION—NOVEMBER 2, 1921

WARREN G. HARDING

JAMES M. COX

1850   1900   1920

13. In which European city did William Caxton first witness Gutenberg's moveable-type printing press?
    a) Cologne
    b) Mainz
    c) Frankfurt
    d) Birmingham

14. The list of books, first issued in 1559, forbidden by the Catholic Church was known as the
    a) *Index Expurgatorius*
    b) *Index Periculum*
    c) *Index Mortis*
    d) *Index Finger*

15. French king Henry IV issued a famous edict granting religious toleration to the Huguenots from which French city?
    a) Nantes
    b) Narbonne
    c) Nîmes
    d) Nice

16. Which English king gave his royal assent to the Act known as Habeas Corpus?
    a) Charles I
    b) Charles II
    c) James II
    d) George I

17. Losing which battle forced King James II to flee to France?
    a) Boyne
    b) Bosworth Field
    c) Blenheim
    d) Britain

18. Which country was the first to pass a Bill of Rights in 1689?
    a) England
    b) France
    c) United States
    d) Russia

19. Russian monarch Peter the Great introduced a tax on which one of the following?
    a) Beards
    b) Pets
    c) Fur
    d) Cheese

20. Laura Bassi, Europe's first female professor, was offered a post at which European university?
    a) Oxford
    b) Rome
    c) Birmingham
    d) Bologna

21. American colonists who protested against paying taxes to Britain in an event known as the Boston Tea Party were disguised as
    a) Clowns
    b) Native Americans
    c) Cowboys
    d) Porters

22. When the 13 American colonies declared their independence from Britain they outlined the right of all men to 'life, liberty and the pursuit of ...'
    a) Wealth
    b) Happiness
    c) Freedom
    d) Love

23. Where did members of the Third Estate (the common people) meet after being barred from an audience with the French king in 1789?
    a) Under the Arc de Triomphe
    b) Inside Notre Dame
    c) Along the Champs-Élysées
    d) On a tennis court

24. Which freedom fighter is sometimes known as 'El Libertador'?
    a) Simón Bolívar
    b) William Wilberforce
    c) Jean-Jacques Dessalines
    d) Spartacus

FREEDOM OF CITIES
(Clause 13)

THE CITY OF LONDON shall have all the old liberties and customs which it hath been used to have. Moreover we will and grant, that all other cities, boroughs, towns, and the barons of the five ports, as with all other ports, shall have all their liberties and free customs.

JUSTICE
(Clauses 39, 40 & 45)

NO FREE MAN shall be seized or imprisoned, or stripped of his rights or possessions, or outlawed or exiled, or deprived of his standing in any way, nor will we proceed with force against him, or send others to do so, except by the lawful judgment of his equals or by the law of the land. ...To no one will we sell, to no one deny or delay right or justice. ... We will appoint as justices, constables, sheriffs, or other officials, only men that know the law of the realm and are minded to keep it well.

LIMITS ON ROYAL POWER
(Clause 61)

THE BARONS shall elect twenty-five of their number to keep, and cause to be observed with all their might, the peace and liberties granted and confirmed to them by this charter.

Photo Credit © Salisbury Cathedral

GALILEO GALILEI
Astronomer

EDWIN SANDYS
Lawyer

JOHN LOCKE
Philosopher

THE EDICT OF NANTES
- 1598 -

FRENCH KING HENRY IV issues an edict granting freedom from persecution to the Huguenots. His bid to restore unity helps end three decades of religious wars in France

PETITION OF RIGHT
-1628-

DISPUTES BETWEEN Parliament and King Charles I lead to a declaration which restricts royal powers over taxation, imprisonment without trial, enforced billeting of soldiers and the use of martial law

GLORIOUS REVOLUTION
- 1688 -

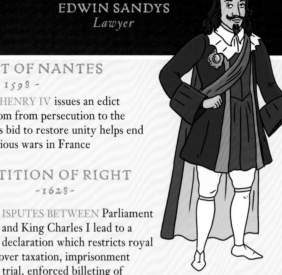

KING JAMES II of England is overthrown by Parliamentarians and Dutch forces led by William of Orange. He later escapes to France in a boat after losing the Battle of the Boyne

GALILEO GALILEI
- 1630 -

ITALIAN SCIENTIST Galileo publicly supports the idea that the Earth goes round the Sun, contradicting Church teaching that the Earth is stationary at the centre of the Universe. Pope Urban VIII puts Galileo under house arrest for heresy

THE LEVELLERS
1647 - 1649

ENGLISH PROTESTORS present An Agreement of the People advocating the idea of popular sovereignty

HABEAS CORPUS & BILL OF RIGHTS
1679 & 1689

FREE SPEECH in Parliament, fair trials before imprisonment (Habeas Corpus), regular elections and the right to petition without fear of reprisal are established in English law for the first time

JOHN LOCKE
- 1689 -

ENGLISH PHILOSOPHER John Locke publishes his *Two Treatises of Government* in which the idea of natural, inalienable rights is described as a social contract between individuals and the state. His work inspires American revolutionaries in the run-up to US independence

THE TREATY OF WESTPHALIA
-1648 -

THE IDEA that European nations may individually choose their own form of government and religion is finally established after thirty years of bitter war in Europe

INDEX EXPURGATORIUS
- 1559 -

POPE PAUL IV issues a list of forbidden books in an attempt to stifle freedom of expression. It goes through 300 editions and is not officially abolished until 1966 by Pope Paul VI

VIRGINIA CHARTER
1606 - 1618

JAMES I signs the Virginia Charter for the purposes of settling the North American continent and making money. Colonists establish the town of Jamestown in 1607, the first permanent English-speaking settlement in the New World. The charter is issued in 1606 and reissued in 1609, 1612 and 1618, promising colonists will enjoy "all Liberties, Franchises, and Immunities ... as if they had been abiding and born, within this our Realm of England". The 1618 edition, drafted by English lawyer Sir Edwin Sandys, guarantees self-government, freedom of speech, equality before the law and trial by jury

BEARD TAX
- 1698 -

RUSSIAN MONARCH Peter the Great tries to model his country on European ideals, banning forced marriages and introducing a tax for people who wear traditional beards

JOAN D'ARC
Freedom fighter

JOHANNES GUTENBERG
Goldsmith and printer

MARTIN LUTHER
Monk

JACK CADE'S REVOLT
- 1450 -

THE BIGGEST ENGLISH uprising of the fifteenth century is led by Kentish rebel Jack Cade. People are enraged at the levels of debt caused by years of war with France and the abuses of power surrounding King Henry VI and his close advisers and allies. Cade leads an anti-corruption march on London. In Shakespeare's play *Henry VI, Part 2*, the rebels, led by Cade, agree that the first thing they will do is "kill all the lawyers"

REFORMATION
- 1517 -

GERMAN MONK Martin Luther objects to the Pope's monopoly over the interpretation of Christian doctrine by nailing 95 objections on the doors of All Saints' Church, Wittenberg. It triggers a reformation in Western Christianity, eventually leading to personal freedoms over the choice and style of religious worship

JOAN D'ARC
- 1431 -

FRENCH FORCES STRUGGLE for liberation against English invasion but their fortunes in the Hundred Years War are transformed by a young peasant girl, the Maid of Orleans. She is eventually captured by English fighters who burn her at the stake as a heretic. Considered as a heroine by the French, she is later made a saint. A statue is erected in her honour outside the church at Bouvines, near Lille

THE BONFIRE OF THE VANITIES
- 1497 -

DOMINICAN FRIAR Girolamo Savonarola leads a revolt in Florence, Italy, against clerical abuses and papal corruption. His supporters burn thousands of books and works of art, mirrors, cosmetics and other artefacts deemed to be decadent and immoral

WILLIAM CAXTON
- 1476 -

ENGLISH MERCHANT William Caxton introduces Gutenberg's moveable-type printing press to England, having seen it in use in Cologne. He establishes a press at Westminster, London. Amongst his first printed books is an edition of Geoffrey Chaucer's *The Canterbury Tales*

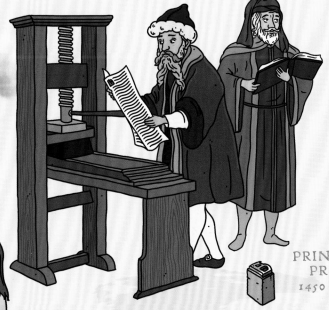

PRINTING PRESS
1450 - 1480

GERMAN GOLDSMITH Johannes Gutenberg pioneers a new cost-effective system for printing books. His moveable-type press uses technology from wine-making and varnish as ink. As a result books can be printed cheaply by anyone with a printing press, removing the power of aristocrats, governments and ecclesiastical authorities to control the flow of words and ideas amongst the general population

25. In 1822 Bill Burns was fined for being cruel to a
  a) Slave
  b) Child
  c) Woman
  d) Donkey

26. Which evil was once described as "bloody traffic"?
  a) Trade in ivory
  b) Trade in slaves
  c) Internment without trial
  d) Driving on the M25

27. In what year was the trade and transport of slaves banned in Britain?
  a) 1807
  b) 1812
  c) 1822
  d) 1833

28. The Education Act of 1870 was championed by which political party?
  a) Liberal
  b) Labour
  c) Conservative
  d) Monster Raving Loony

29. Hundreds of thousands of people celebrated what in 1886 in New York City?
  a) The opening of the New York subway
  b) The completion of the world's tallest skyscraper
  c) The unveiling of the Statue of Liberty
  d) The first 'freedom' bagel

30. What is the motto for the General Federation of Trade Unions?
  a) Unity is strength
  b) Strength in numbers
  c) Workers unite
  d) If you can't beat 'em, join 'em

31. Which famous politician was instrumental in helping pass the Parliament Act of 1911, making the House of Commons the supreme law-making body in the UK?
  a) David Lloyd George
  b) Margaret Thatcher
  c) William Pitt
  d) Winston Churchill

32. Whilst campaigning for women's right to vote suffragette Emily Davison was killed by
  a) A car
  b) A train
  c) A bicycle
  d) A horse

33. What were the initials of Lawrence of Arabia?
  a) T.E.
  b) T.S.
  c) D.H.
  d) K.V.

34. Which of the following amendments to the US Constitution gave women the vote?
  a) 5th
  b) 11th
  c) 14th
  d) 19th

35. Who was the first female MP to take a seat in the House of Commons?
  a) Emmeline Pankhurst
  b) Nancy Astor
  c) Constance Markievicz
  d) Beatrix Potter

36. Which US president's State of the Union address outlined four basic human freedoms: Speech, Religion Want and Fear?
  a) Eisenhower
  b) Kennedy
  c) Hoover
  d) Roosevelt

37. Which of the following countries abstained from voting in favour of the Universal Declaration of Human Rights?
  a) United States of America
  b) France
  c) Greece
  d) Saudi Arabia

38. In 1955 Rosa Parks, a seamstress from Alabama, USA, was arrested after
  a) Driving the wrong way down a one-way street
  b) Sewing the wrong buttons on the president's jacket
  c) Protesting against a ban on women drivers
  d) Refusing to give up her seat on a bus

39. US civil rights leader Martin Luther King made his most famous speech in 1963, immortalised with the words ...
  a) I have a vision
  b) I have a dream
  c) I have an idea
  d) I have a plan

THE MAGNA CARTA CHRONICLE

This commemorative book has been produced
with generous funding and support from the Magna Carta 800th Committee,
established to co-ordinate the 800th centenary commemorations
of the sealing of Magna Carta.

It has been written, designed, illustrated and produced by
What on Earth Publishing, specialists in the art of telling stories through timelines.

For more information, please visit

www.magnacarta800th.com
www.whatonearthbooks.com/magnacarta

THE MAGNA CARTA CHRONICLE

SIMON DE MONTFORT, a crusader against the A
in France, issues a set of
that create precedents for Ma
especially in establishing the f
the Church from royal interfe

KING AETHELBERHT
- 604 -

ANGLO-SAXON King Aethelberht of Kent creates the first English code of laws that establishes the principle of punishments by financial penalty rather than by blood feuds. His codified (as opposed to retributive) laws mark a turning point in the history of legal systems

CYRUS CYLINDER
- 539 BC -

DESCRIBED as 'the first charter of human rights', this 2,600-year-old artefact, discovered in the ruins of Babylon in 1879, tells how Persian king Cyrus the Great freed people from captivity after his conquest of Babylon

ASHOKA'S EDICTS
- 240 BC -

INDIAN KING ASHOKA is so appalled at the horrors of war that he makes a series of 33 inscriptions on pillars across his empire which detail a range of moral laws. They include kindness to prisoners, respect for animals, tolerance for all religions and hospitality to travellers

THE CHARTER OF LIBERTIES
- 1100 -

THIS CHARTER is sealed by King Henry I at his coronation. For the first time since the Norman Conquest of 1066, English barons seek to curtail the monarch's power to raise arbitrary taxes and sell offices of Church and State

FOL
Joh
of F
He reissue
edition of
the accessi
of nine-yea
Henry III

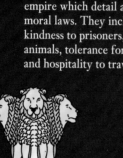

LAWS OF HAMMURABI
- 1754 BC -

THE OLDEST surviving legal code is inscribed on a stone pillar in ncient Babylon. Its 282 laws over everything from ontracts and wages to family isputes, inheritance and ivorce. Slaves and peasants re punished more harshly than eople of higher social standing nd punishments follow a etributive model of 'An eye or an eye, a tooth for a tooth'

SPARTACUS REVOLT
- 73 BC -

ESCAPED GLADIATOR Spartacus leads a revolt of more than 70,000 slaves against oppressive Roman rule. Although they are defeated by Roman general Crassus (who crucifies 6,000 prisoners on the roadside between Capua and Rome), their protest inspires freedom fighters for thousands of years

MAGNA CARTA
- 1215 issue -

ON JUNE 15, having failed in the previous year to regain Normandy at the Battle of Bouvines, King John is cornered in the water meadow at Runnymede and agrees to a peace treaty with rebellious barons. The charter, influenced by Archbishop Stephen Langton, guarantees the freedom of the Church from royal interference and limits the power of the King to raise taxes without permission from his nobles. A council of 25 barons is appointed to oversee its provisions

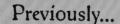

STEPHEN LANGTON
Archbishop of Canterbury

SIMON DE MONTFORT
Baronial rebel

WAT TYLER
Revolting peasant

GOLDEN BULL
- 1222 -

IN AN ECHO of Magna Carta, Hungarian King Andrew II is forced by his nobles to issue an edict limiting his royal powers. The edict establishes the principle that all nobles are equal

[MA]GNA CARTA
- 1216 issue -

[FOLLO]WING THE DEATH of King [William] Marshal, 1st Earl [... broke,] becomes regent. [... a] slightly revised [Ma]gnaCarta on [... to] the throne [... o]ld King

FIRST REPRESENTATIVE PARLIAMENT
- 1265 -

A GROUP OF rebellious barons, led by Simon de Montfort the younger, gathers without the King's approval in what is regarded as the first-ever representative parliament. Two elected knights from each county and two burgesses from each borough are sent as participants. It is the first political gathering to include commoners

PEASANTS' REVOLT
- 1381 -

KENTISH REBELS advance on London, led by roofer Wat Tyler and priest John Ball, who preaches that all people should be treated equally. The peasants protest against taxes imposed by King Richard II to finance his wars against France. The revolt fizzles out after Tyler is decapitated by the King's supporters during negotiations at Smithfield in London

MAGNA CARTA
- 1225 issue -

HENRY III reissues Magna Carta and the Charter of the Forest as a result of his need to raise taxes. For the first time Magna Carta clearly contains the connection to 'no taxation without representation'

SUMPTUARY LAW
- 1363 -

A LAW IS PASSED by the English Parliament decreeing the quality and colour of cloth peasants are allowed to wear. Such measures indicate growing social mobility amongst the lower classes

MAGNA CARTA
- 1217 issue -

MAGNA CARTA is reissued once again, following the defeat of French invaders at the Battle of Lincoln. It is issued alongside a new charter dealing with the royal forest. The name Magna Carta appears for the first time in a proclamation in February of the following year

MAGNA CARTA
- 1297 issue -

EDWARD I REISSUES Magna Carta in return for baronial support for taxes to fund English wars against France. This issue of Magna Carta is entered into the English Statute Book for the first time and thus becomes enshrined into English law

BLACK DEATH
1348-1350

AS MANY AS 200 million people worldwide die from a bacterial disease carried by rats and transmitted by fleas. Originating in Asia, the disease spreads across Europe, reaching England in 1348. Peasants, labourers and artisans are worst hit but those who survive are gradually able to demand higher wages, helping bring an end to the age of feudalism

40. Computer whizz Alan Turing took his own life after receiving
   a) A Nobel Peace Prize
   b) A knighthood
   c) Hormone therapy
   d) A Sinclair ZX81

41. Which famous politician described the divide between Eastern and Western Europe as an Iron Curtain?
   a) Winston Churchill
   b) Enoch Powell
   c) John F. Kennedy
   d) Margaret Thatcher

42. People who took chipped-off parts of the Berlin Wall to keep as souvenirs were known as
   a) Chipolatas
   b) Blockheads
   c) Wallies
   d) Wall Woodpeckers

43. The Church of England's parliament is known as the
   a) General Election
   b) General Synod
   c) General Consensus
   d) General Knowledge

44. Who was Archbishop of Canterbury at the time when the Church of England first allowed the ordination of women?
   a) Robert Runcie
   b) Rowan Williams
   c) George Carey
   d) George Clooney

45. How many years did Nelson Mandela spend in prison?
   a) 13
   b) 17
   c) 22
   d) 27

46. The European Court of Human Rights is based in which city?
   a) Strasbourg
   b) Brussels
   c) The Hague
   d) Geneva

47. Fruit and vegetable seller Mohamed Bouazizi set himself on fire in protest against the government of which country?
   a) Syria
   b) Egypt
   c) Saudi Arabia
   d) Tunisia

48. Sir Tim Berners-Lee invented what?
   a) The iPhone
   b) The World Wide Web
   c) Facebook
   d) Worcestershire Sauce

49. What percentage of the Scottish electorate turned out to vote in the 2014 independence referendum?
   a) 35%
   b) 65%
   c) 85%
   d) 97%

50. How old was Malala Yousafzai when she won the Nobel Peace Prize?
   a) 14
   b) 16
   c) 17
   d) 19

All the correct answers can be found somewhere inside the book or on the timeline overleaf.
Alternatively, you can request a copy of the answers by emailing
magnaquiz@whatonearthbooks.com